FIGHTER JETS

John Willis

AV2

www.openlightbox.com

AV2

Step 1
Go to **www.openlightbox.com**

Step 2
Enter this unique code
TMOLNBOG7

Step 3
Explore your interactive eBook!

AV2 is optimized for use on any device

Your interactive eBook comes with...

- **Audio** (Read) — Listen to the entire book read aloud
- **Videos** — Watch informative video clips
- **Weblinks** — Gain additional information for research
- **Try This!** — Complete activities and hands-on experiments
- **Key Words** — Study vocabulary, and complete a matching word activity
- **Quizzes** — Test your knowledge
- **Slideshows** — View images and captions
- **Share** — Share titles within your Learning Management System (LMS) or Library Circulation System
- **Citation** — Create bibliographical references following APA, CMOS, and MLA styles

This title is part of our AV2 digital subscription

1-Year K–5 Subscription
ISBN 978-1-7911-3320-7

Access hundreds of AV2 titles with our digital subscription.
Sign up for a FREE trial at **www.openlightbox.com/trial**

The digital components of this book are guaranteed to stay active for at least five years from the date of publication.

MEGA MILITARY MACHINES

FIGHTER JETS

CONTENTS

Fighter jets are very fast airplanes. The United States Air Force, Navy, and Marine Corps use them.

COMPARING FIGHTER JET NUMBERS

Marine Corps

About **290** fighter jets

Navy

About **530** fighter jets

Air Force

About **1,160** fighter jets

Airplanes must move forward to fly. Fighter jets have jet engines to help move them forward.

Jet engines use a large amount of fuel very quickly. This makes it hard for fighter jets to stay in the air for long periods of time.

COMPARING FUEL USAGE

Medium-sized Private Jet
About **4 gallons per minute** (15 liters per minute)

Passenger Plane
About **60 gallons per minute** (230 lpm)

Fighter Jet
About **385 gallons per minute** (1,460 lpm)

Fighter jets use tankers to refuel without having to land.

Fighter jets have a tool called radar. It helps pilots find other planes from far away.

COMM 1
COMM 2
VOL
CLR
ENT
SVE
I/P
IFF
TCN
AWL
BCN
ALT
LANDING
DAY
NGT
CONT
BINGO
BRAKE

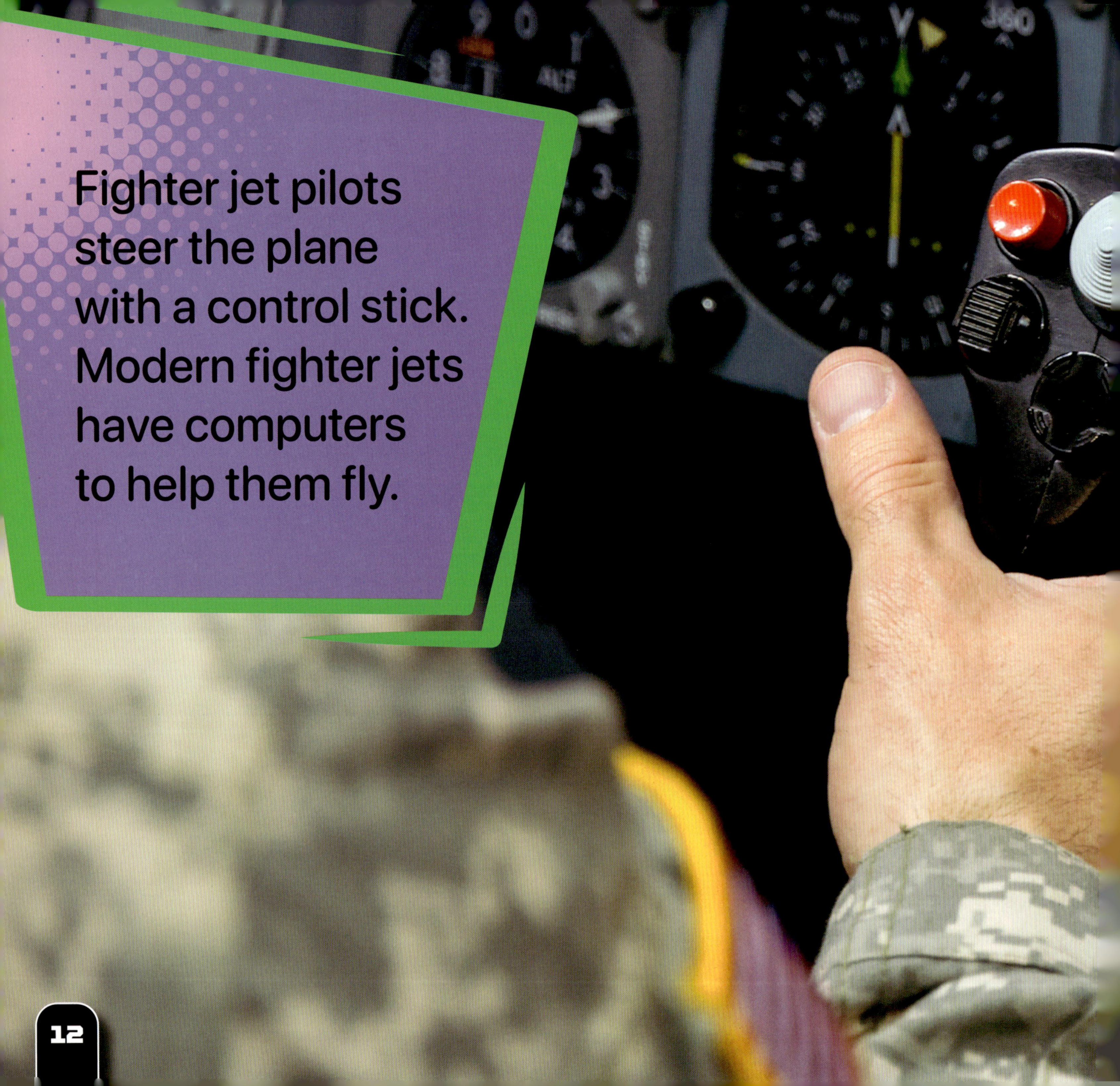

Fighter jet pilots steer the plane with a control stick. Modern fighter jets have computers to help them fly.

TBT
C x100
CNT
BRT
CANCEL OVR
MSL ARM
SEL
NORM
AUTO
RATE
GUN ARM

The first fighter jet the U.S. Air Force used for missions was the F-80 Shooting Star.

FAMOUS FIGHTER JETS

1945

F-80 Shooting Star

1978

F-16 Fighting Falcon

2005

F-22 Raptor

More than 1,700 F-80 Shooting Stars were built for the U.S. military.

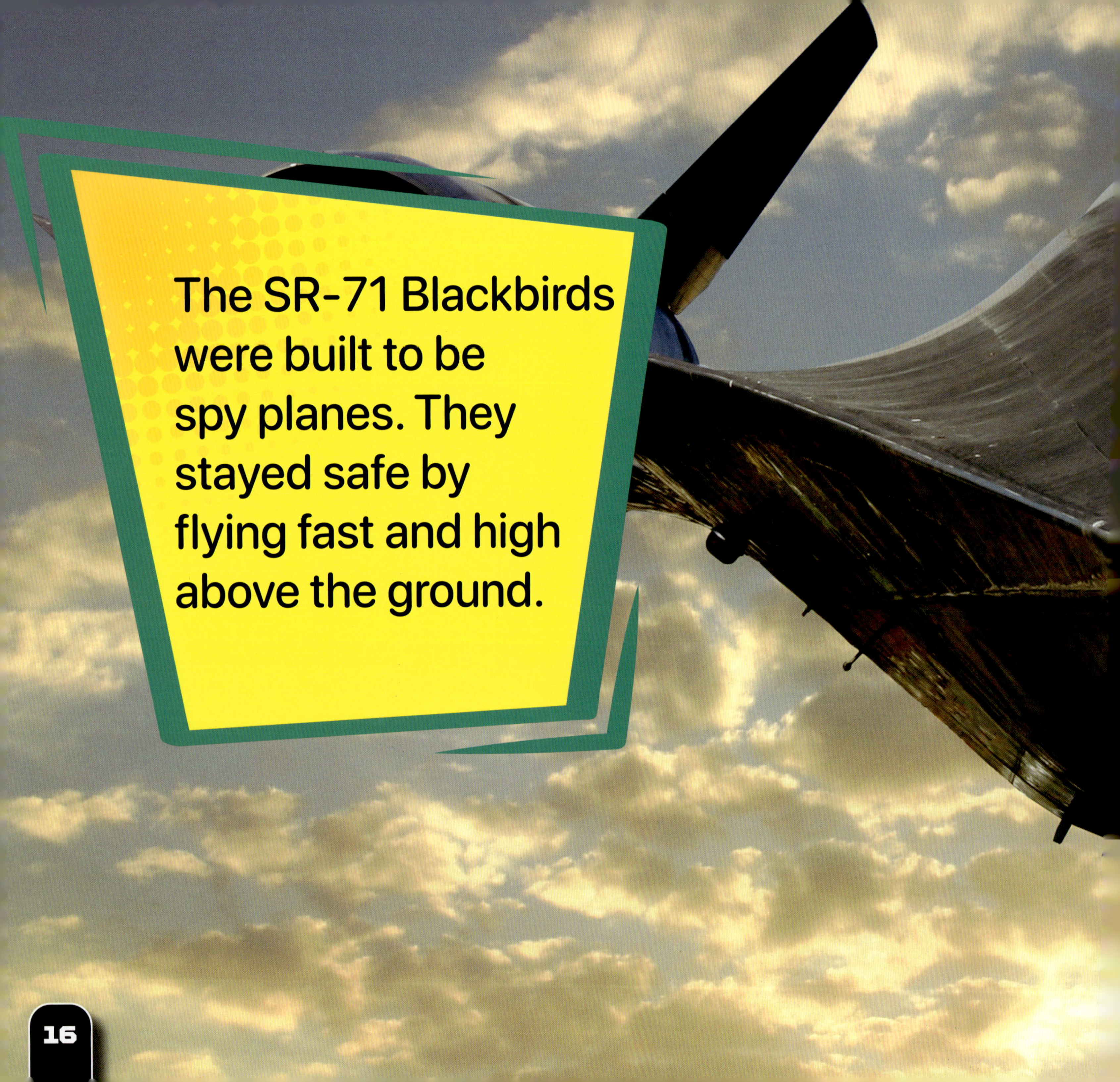

The SR-71 Blackbirds were built to be spy planes. They stayed safe by flying fast and high above the ground.

These spy planes could travel at more than three times the speed of sound.

Most planes need a runway to take off, but some fighter jets can lift straight up. They can hover like a helicopter.

Flying a fighter jet can be dangerous. Fighter jets have special features to keep pilots safe.

See what you have learned about fighter jets.

Which of these pictures does not show a fighter jet?

KEY WORDS

Research has shown that as much as 65 percent of all written material published in English is made up of 300 words. These 300 words cannot be taught using pictures or learned by sounding them out. They must be recognized by sight. This book contains 59 common sight words to help young readers improve their reading fluency and comprehension. This book also teaches young readers several important content words, such as proper nouns. These words are paired with pictures to aid in learning and improve understanding.

Page	Sight Words First Appearance
4	air, and, are, states, the, them, use, very
5	about, numbers
7	have, help, move, must, to
8	a, for, hard, in, it, large, long, makes, of, this, time
9	land, without
10	away, far, find, from, other
12	with
14	first, was
15	more, than, were
16	above, be, by, high, they
17	at, could, sound, these, three
18	but, can, like, most, need, off, some, take, up
20	keep

Page	Content Words First Appearance
4	Air Force, airplanes, fighter jets, Marine Corps, Navy, United States
7	jet engines
8	amount, fuel, gallons, liters, minute, passenger plane, periods, private jet, usage
9	tankers
10	pilots, radar, tool
12	computers, control stick
14	F-16 Fighting Falcon, F-22 Raptor, F-80 Shooting Star, missions
15	military
16	ground, spy planes, SR-71 Blackbirds
18	helicopter, runway
20	features

Published by Lightbox Learning Inc.
276 5th Avenue, Suite 704 #917
New York, NY 10001
Website: www.openlightbox.com

Library of Congress Control Number: 2023931794

ISBN 978-1-7911-5535-3 (hardcover)
ISBN 978-1-7911-5536-0 (softcover)
ISBN 978-1-7911-5537-7 (multi-user eBook)

Printed in Guangzhou, China
1 2 3 4 5 6 7 8 9 0 27 26 25 24 23

042023
100922

Project Coordinator: Priyanka Das **Designer:** Terry Paulhus

Every reasonable effort has been made to trace ownership and to obtain permission to reprint copyright material. The publisher would be pleased to have any errors or omissions brought to its attention so that they may be corrected in subsequent printings.

The publisher acknowledges Alamy, Dreamstime, Getty Images, Shutterstock, and Wikimedia as the primary image suppliers for this title.